EDWARD WILKINS
and his friend Gwendoline

EDWARD WILKINS
and his friend Gwendoline

BARBARA BOLTON

Illustrated by Madeleine Winch

ANGUS & ROBERTSON PUBLISHERS

"I don't want to watch this junk," said Jason. "Who wants to see a lot of dancing on TV?"

"Not me," said Shane, switching channels.

"Well, I do!" retorted Melanie, switching back to the ballet. "And Mum said I could because you watched that space thing last night. So there!"

I sat on the windowsill, watching them and feeling grumpy.

I am Edward Wilkins, black cat, and I can tell you there's a lot to be said against sharing a house with three young two-legs.

I mean, they are noisy, they are rough and there are times when tails are pulled—which no cat of my age should have to tolerate.

Also, they don't speak a word of cat. Not that I have anything to say to them, *because I don't.*

"We could have another look through Nan's trunk," said Jason. "We might find her jewels."

"No point," said Shane. "We've looked and looked. Anyway, they couldn't be worth much."

I bristled. There was a very nice piece of amber on a thin gold chain; there was an amethyst brooch; there was a silver bracelet; there was a diamond ring. Not worth much, indeed!

Gwendoline was very fond of those jewels. My friend Gwendoline was the children's grandmother. I shared her house until she died a few weeks ago. And I enjoyed living with *her* more than I enjoy living here, I can tell you that much!

I know where the jewels are, of course. There were no secrets between Gwendoline and me.

"I'll put them in the blue biscuit jar," she said. "Anna should have my engagement ring, and she always liked the bracelet and the brooch. Melanie could have the amber pendant. The boys won't want jewellery, so I'll leave two $5 notes for them. You'll see they get them, Edward, won't you?"

I said I would, and if they show me proper respect I dare say I'll eventually point the blue biscuit jar out to them. It's in a box with Gwendoline's teacups and things, but nobody's bothered to look inside it.

"Look at old Edward," grinned Jason now. "He's half asleep. He does nothing *but* sleep."

"He's old," said Shane. "Mum says he could be seventeen. Most cats don't live that long."

"He'll drop dead one of these days," said Jason.

I'll drop dead when I'm good and ready. I opened my eyes and gave him a very cold look.

"Look at him glare," said Jason. "You'd think he knew what we were saying."

Shane laughed rudely and tweaked my tail.

"Ouch!" he yelled, as I caught him with a claw. He grabbed me by the scruff of the neck, but Melanie was on to him like a flash, punching and kicking.

"Leave him alone!" she shouted. "You can't blame Edward. You started it! He was Nan's cat and you leave him alone."

I retired beneath the easy chair and started to wash myself in a thoughtful sort of way. There are times when I think young Melanie shows promise.

Maybe I will teach her some cat language and then I'll be able to tell her how I first went to live with Gwendoline.

It was a cold, wet night in early spring; a wind blowing handfuls of rain against the windowpanes of the houses. I was ill and my fur was wet. I was chilled to the bone.

I padded down a back street in Richmond, searching for shelter. I had no fixed address in those days. I slept wherever it was most convenient. That night nowhere seemed to be convenient.

I prided myself on being able to manage alone. I was a good hunter and I could always catch enough game to feed myself well, but it had been a hard winter and now I was thin and sick.

"If I do not find somewhere for the night," I thought, "I am done for."

Then I saw a small house, very old, very shabby, built flat against the street. I noticed it because the blind was up in the window and a warm yellow light shone through.

Gathering up all my strength I jumped onto the windowsill. I could see an old woman (naturally, I didn't know her name then) sitting in a wicker chair in front of a fire.

It was a dreadful old house, almost falling down. There were cracks in the walls and a big stain on the ceiling, and the floor was uneven. But the flames were leaping and dancing in the fireplace and there was a black kettle sitting on the hob.

I knew if I could get in there I would be safe. Cats have a sense about things like that.

I tapped on the window with my paw. The old woman did not hear. I raised my voice and called. She kept staring into the fire. I wailed, and at last she raised her head and saw me.

I thought at once that she seemed intelligent for a two-leg. I tapped on the window again and Gwendoline hurried to her feet and came to the door and let me in.

Some of the rain and wind came in with me. Gwendoline slammed the door and plugged up a crack or two with newspaper.

"It's not a fit night to be out, puss," she said. "Come in, come in. Sit down by the fire."

I struggled over to the fire and collapsed on the rug. Gwendoline fetched an old towel and rubbed me down. "You're not well, poor puss," she said sympathetically.

"My name is Edward Wilkins," I said. But she spoke no cat at the time, so she did not understand.

"Don't you worry, puss," she went on. "I'll make you better. Warm milk, a dash of honey, a good night's sleep in front of a warm fire—you won't know yourself."

She heated up the milk and dissolved some honey in it. "You can't beat honey," she said, and I took a mouthful or two to please her.

Gwendoline found an old box and lined it with a piece of rug. "Here's a nice bed for you," she said. She picked me up and placed me in the box, very gently.

"If you're not well by the time I draw my pension, old puss," she murmured comfortingly, "I'll take you to a vet."

I remember feeling a little annoyed at being called "old puss". I was around seven at the time and I wasn't old. And I can remember wondering how long it would be until pension day, because I was feeling very ill indeed.

The next few days are all jumbled up in my mind. But I know that Gwendoline was there, every time I woke up. She stroked my fur and fed me on warm milk from a spoon.

At last I was able to sit up to nibble a sardine or two.

"You're looking perkier now, old puss," said Gwendoline.

"I am not old," I responded, nettled. "And my name is Edward Wilkins."

She looked at me with her faded grey eyes. "Sometimes," she said, "you can almost talk."

That was when I first thought of teaching her the cat language. But I did not start there and then.

Indeed, I had no thought of staying. But looking around the old house I could see the signs of mice. Rats as well.

"She has been good to you, Edward Wilkins," I said to myself. "The least you can do is to clear out those mice for her."

I had always enjoyed hunting. I settled myself in and, one by one, I caught those mice. At least, I caught nine, and then they passed the word around (as mice do) and decided to move on to other lodgings.

Every time I caught a mouse I would take it to Gwendoline and lay it out before her. "Good cat," she would say, looking at the mouse with interest. No screaming, no fussing. I liked her more and more.

Out in the street the plane trees budded; the leaves grew and spread. I had started on the rats now and by the time summer came they had decided to move on, too.

"You're worth your weight in gold, puss," said Gwendoline.

I was tired of being called "puss". It is not a name I care for. So I started teaching her cat during the summer evenings—and I must say I never had a better pupil. Not that I had had many, because, generally speaking, cats don't teach two-legs their language.

"It's astonishing," Gwendoline said. "I had a ginger cat for nine years and he never taught me this, Edward."

He wouldn't. Ginger cats make particularly poor teachers. No patience.

Autumn came. The mornings were frosty. At night Gwendoline built up the fire.

"Stay for the winter," she begged me. "We'd be company for one another."

I thought of her spending the long winter nights alone and I hadn't the heart to leave her. "I will stay until spring comes," I said.

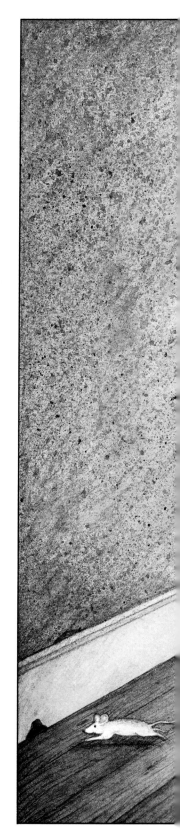

And so, little by little, I settled in. By spring another family of rats had moved in and I had to stay to clean them out. By summer I had started to teach Gwendoline the languages of the Persian and Siamese cats (you never know when it will come in useful to know a foreign language) and she was telling me how she had once nearly landed a starring role in a musical comedy.

By autumn Gwendoline had made such good progress with Siamese and Persian that I could see it would be a sin to leave without starting her on tabby. You rarely find a two-leg who can master tabby, and I wanted to see whether she could manage it.

"It's the intonation," she complained. "That's what I find hard. Of course, I was never a singer, Edward, and I dare say that accounts for it. It held me back in my career. If I'd had a voice as good as my legs I would have gone a good deal further."

"It is always as well," I said, "to have more than one string to your bow. My old mother used to say to me, 'Edward, you can be a mouser or a ratter, but it's best to be able to turn your paw to either.' "

For by that time I was telling Gwendoline about my life as a kitten on the fishing boat *Nancy Jane*.

My mother had told me about the night I was born . . .

"It was a wild, wet night," she began. "Old Gubbins, the owner of the boat, had been celebrating his own birthday. He'd finished off a bottle of rum, and the three of you were two days old before he felt well enough to name you." (I should say here that often a mother cat living with a two-leg allows the two-leg to name her kittens. The two-legs enjoy such things and it does no harm to the kittens.)

"He called the females Esmeralda and Ermyntrude," my mother went on, remembering, "and he called you Edward. He told me I could keep you for company, but the females would have to go ashore as soon as they could manage for themselves."

"And so they went," I said. "Where did they go ashore?"

"At a little port," my mother said. "A sleepy town up the coast. I've heard since that it's a good place for cats. Old Gubbins took the girls over in the dinghy and left them at a house with white violets growing by the gate. He said it looked like a friendly place, and I suppose it was."

So I was left as my mother's only companion, apart from old Gubbins who was drunk so often you couldn't properly count *him* as company.

Soon she was teaching me her trade.

For my mother was known far and wide as a ratter and mouser beyond compare. She prided herself on having the fastest claw on the coast.

"A cat needs to be independent, Edward," she would say. "You need to be able to catch your own food, and don't you ever forget it."

I enjoyed learning the trade. My mother taught me Stalking and Pouncing and put me through a special course on Smelling Out the Game.

She insisted that I practise and practise until I had a firm grip on the essentials—including the mouse.

I think she was proud of me. "You remind me of myself at your age," she said. "I *may* have been a little faster than you, but you're shaping up well, young Edward."

But the time came when she felt like having the boat to herself again. (Catwise, I mean. Old Gubbins was still aboard, of course.)

"No hard feelings, Edward," she explained. "But I've taught you all I know and the truth is that I'm a cat who likes to be alone a good deal of the time."

"Fair enough," I said. "And in any case I fancy seeing something of the city."

So at the next port I went ashore and set out for Melbourne. It was a long walk, and I stopped off here and there, staying at a likely barn or house for a few months at a time. But eventually I arrived in the big city and never regretted the move.

Born at sea I may have been, but at heart I am a city cat. I like streets and lanes, buildings, houses and warehouses (you get marvellous hunting in warehouses). I like the grass and dandelions that grow on vacant blocks. I like the feeling that I am in a city where millions of cats roam. You can meet a new one every day if you want to. Or, on the other hand, you can choose to stay alone. Oh yes, I enjoy the city thoroughly.

Well, as I've already said, I eventually found Gwendoline. We suited one another. From time to time I went my way and she went hers. But we always enjoyed getting back together again and having a good talk about what had happened.

I remember the time that she told me she was thinking of moving.

"This place is falling down around me, Edward," she said. "The landlord won't lift a finger to do anything about it, make no mistake about *that*. And I've heard I can put my name down for a flat."

"How big?" I asked.

"Bed-sitting room, small bathroom, kitchenette," she said. "Everything we need. Hot water supplied, central heating in winter. There's only one problem."

"And what is that?" I asked.

"The rules," she said quietly. "No pets allowed."

I thought for a moment.

"I am not a pet," I pointed out. "I am an independent cat who lives with you, paying his own way by mousing and ratting, catching a lot of his own food. That is not a pet."

"Very true," said Gwendoline. "I'll put my name down tomorrow and I won't say a word about you."

"That will be best," I agreed, licking my fur and thinking that they could have worse tenants than me.

We waited two years for the flat as things turned out, and by the time we were told we could move our roof was leaking badly and the floor had rotted away in part of the lounge room.

"I tell you," said Gwendoline, on our first night in the flat, "that building would have fallen down around us, Edward. We're lucky to get out."

I was not so sure about that at first. I had come with her because we were friends, but like most cats I did not care too much for new territory.

I mean, I had staked out my claim to a certain area in *South* Richmond. All the other cats in the area knew me and knew where I stood on such issues as hunting rights and seasons and so on.

Now we had moved to *North* Richmond, and no-one knew me there. I had to start establishing myself all over again.

But slowly I became fond of the flat. We were very proud of it and kept it like a new pin. There was no open fire, but it was very cosy in winter all the same.

It was a ground-floor flat and we had a little garden at our door. A pink geranium grew there and Gwendoline planted some daffodil bulbs and a root of lily-of-the-valley.

"We never had much of a garden in the house where I lived as a child," she said. "We lived on the shady side of the street and my mother never did much gardening. But lily-of-the-valley grew wild there and in spring the scent was like something out of heaven."

Well, perhaps it was. What Gwendoline had forgotten was that our garden was on the *sunny* side of the street and our lily-of-the-valley showed no inclination at all to grow wild. But it put up a few leaves, and in spring there was sometimes a stalk or two of flowers.

The flats were free of mice and rats, and I was able to take life quietly. I was not sorry, to tell the truth. I was not as young as I used to be, no two ways about that, and I was glad to be able to spend time lying out in the sun in our little garden, dreaming about the past. Often, too, I would sit beside Gwendoline's chair, chatting with her about her career on the stage and her grandchildren and one thing and another.

Sometimes we talked two-leg, sometimes we talked cat. Either way we enjoyed discussing life and sharing our views.

But gradually I noticed that Gwendoline was talking more and more about the day she would die.

"I'm getting old, Edward," she sighed, "and I'm tired. I won't be sorry to go. I've arranged for you to live with my daughter and her children. You'll enjoy that, won't you?"

Knowing her grandchildren I thought it most unlikely I would enjoy it. But manners are manners.

"Very nice," I said.

Winter came, and Gwendoline talked about the spring, and about dying. "I would like to see the daffodils again," she said. "I would like to smell the lily-of-the-valley. But there you are. We can't live forever. And I believe in heaven, Edward. I've always believed in that. I expect I'll like it there."

"What is it like?" I asked, thinking of it as another part of the city, maybe over in the distance where at night-time the lights flashed and twinkled.

"Streets of gold, they say," said Gwendoline, "and gates of pearl. It should be quite nice."

She looked around our little flat. We had a patchwork quilt on her bed and a wicker chair for her. There was a brown cushion in my box-bed.

We had a pot-plant stand with three tiers and there we grew two ferns, an ivy, an African violet and a red tulip.

There was a large photo of Gwendoline's husband (about whom she rarely spoke) and an old, faded picture of her parents.

"Of course," she said, "it's nice here—if it comes to that."

"But you are tired?" I asked.

"I'm tired and I'm old," she answered. "That's what it is, Edward. I'll be glad to go to heaven. They say you're always young in heaven."

"You will dance again," I said.

Her eyes brightened. "I'll like that," said Gwendoline.

She leant back in her wicker chair and pulled her rug over her knees. She was always cold that last winter.

"Only one thing worries me," she said. "And that's you, Edward. I'd like to think you'd come and join me. But I've never heard of a cat going to heaven."

"Have you ever heard of a cat *not* going to heaven?" I asked. "Have you heard of one being turned away from the gates?"

"No," she said. "I've never heard of one being turned away."

"The point is, of course," I reasoned, "most cats would not *want* to go to heaven. I do not know that I want to go there myself."

I have never seen streets of gold before and I am not sure that I fancy them. I am not sure that I fancy gates of pearl, either. I have never lived in a place like that.

"I would miss you, Gwendoline," I said, "but I do not know that I want to go to heaven."

"I hope you do come, Edward," she said. "I don't want to be without you."

Well, there came a day when she died. Very quietly, while she was sleeping. I knew almost at once that she was dead and I stayed beside her very patiently, waiting for someone to come.

"Do not worry, Gwendoline," I said. "I will come to heaven if you want me to come. I will not stay long away."

Our neighbours called Gwendoline's daughter and I was brought home to this place. It is not what I am used to. Noise all the time. And they never buy me sardines.

But they are Gwendoline's family and I must make the best of it. And I am starting to see good points in Melanie.

One day soon I may show them where the jewellery is hidden. I may even teach Melanie a little cat, some basic black cat perhaps, and *tell* her where it is to be found. I think Gwendoline would like Melanie to be the first to know.

And then, when I have done that, it will be time for me to go and be with Gwendoline.

Streets of gold . . . I suppose one gets used to them.

And maybe it won't be so bad. After all, Gwendoline will be there.

It will be good to see her dance . . . I never knew Gwendoline in her dancing days.

Oh, if Gwendoline is in heaven I will be content.

"They say we'll have mansions up there," she said once. "How about that, Edward? At one time I had a friend who promised to build me a mansion, but he never did. Maybe I'll get that mansion in heaven."

But I don't care about a mansion. All I really ask for is a warm room with a wicker chair for Gwendoline and a box for me. Gwendoline probably has those things all ready. She's been there long enough now to get settled in.

I shall walk straight up to the gates of heaven and call to be let in. When the gates open, in I will go, my tail high and my head up.

I hope they will be able to speak cat. Gwendoline said she believed all languages were spoken there.

"I have come to join Gwendoline," I will say. "Tell her Edward Wilkins, black cat, is here."

I dare say she will have a bowl of milk waiting for me.